HOT CIDER, HOT ___ AND HOT FLAS___

Maxine's Guide to the Holidays

Illustrated by:
John M. Wagner

A Shoebox Greetings Book
(A tiny, little division of Hallmark)
Andrews and McMeel
A Universal Press Syndicate Company
Kansas City

*To Kari ann
from Mom dar
Love*

Other SHOEBOX GREETINGS Books
from Andrews and McMeel

SHOEBOX GREETINGS
(A tiny little division of Hallmark)

Crabby Road
Don't Worry, Be Crabby
Raiders of the Lost Bark
Workin' Noon to Five
The Mom Dictionary

WRITTEN BY:

Chris Brethwaite
Bill Bridgeman
Bill Gray
Allyson Jones
Kevin Kinzer
Mark Oatman

Scott Oppenheimer
Dee Ann Stewart
Dan Taylor
Rich Warwick
Myra Zirkle

ISBN: 0-8362-2192-3

Library of Congress Catalog Card Number: 96-84112

ATTENTION: SCHOOLS AND BUSINESSES

Andrews and McMeel books are available at quantity discounts with bulk purchase for educational, business, or sales promotional use. For information, write to: Special Sales Department, Andrews and McMeel, 4520 Main Street, Kansas City, Missouri 64111.

The weather outside is
frightful?

Well stay inside,
Sherlock!

What's more fun than catching a snowflake on your tongue?

Actually, just about anything.

Christmas finds me with a song in my heart. It's a little-known ditty called, "Oh, Leave Me Alone and Maybe I Won't Hurt You."

'Tis the season to be jolly!

If you're a conglomerate that owns several major department stores, a few discount chains, a mega-mall or two...

Ever notice how postal employees apparently think "Fragile" means "Drop-kick this sucker into the big pile in the back of the truck?"
"Rattle"
"Rattle"
"Rattle"

It's Christmastime in the city!
So, I'm thinking of moving to the country.

Ah, the holidays, when the earth is covered with a beautiful, thick dusting of white stuff from above.

Reminds me of my lapels.

This year I'm only
buying gifts for the
ones I really like.

So that would pretty
much be myself,
my dog and the cat.

29

At Christmastime, I like to do a little something for the mailman and the paperboy.

This year I might keep the dog tied up.

It's Christmas!

Time to see which family member is scratching himself in the group photos.

There's nothing like the sight of a pale moon after a snowfall!
It's even worth risking a frostbitten butt!

At Christmastime, it's
   fun to surprise people who
      weren't expecting anything!

A slushball to the back
   of the head surprises
      just about everybody!

There's nothing I like better than Shooshing down a frozen hill on a toboggan!
...and slamming into a shopper loaded down with packages at the bottom.

Feel that chill in the air?
Seems like a good time to sneak up behind strangers and snap their earmuffs against the sides of their heads.

January often finds me paying bills by the flickering firelight.

Maybe this year I'll get to the electric bill first.

70

Christmas is coming, the geese are getting fat.

I must be related to a lot of geese.

I always remember my paper boy at the holidays.

I remember all the times he threw my paper in the bushes.

There are really only five days of Christmas.

It just seems like twelve when you have relatives staying with you.

I always exchange names with the relatives at Christmas.

They call me "Crabby." I call them "Buttheads"... they call me "Whinebag." I call them "Mouth-breathers"...

83

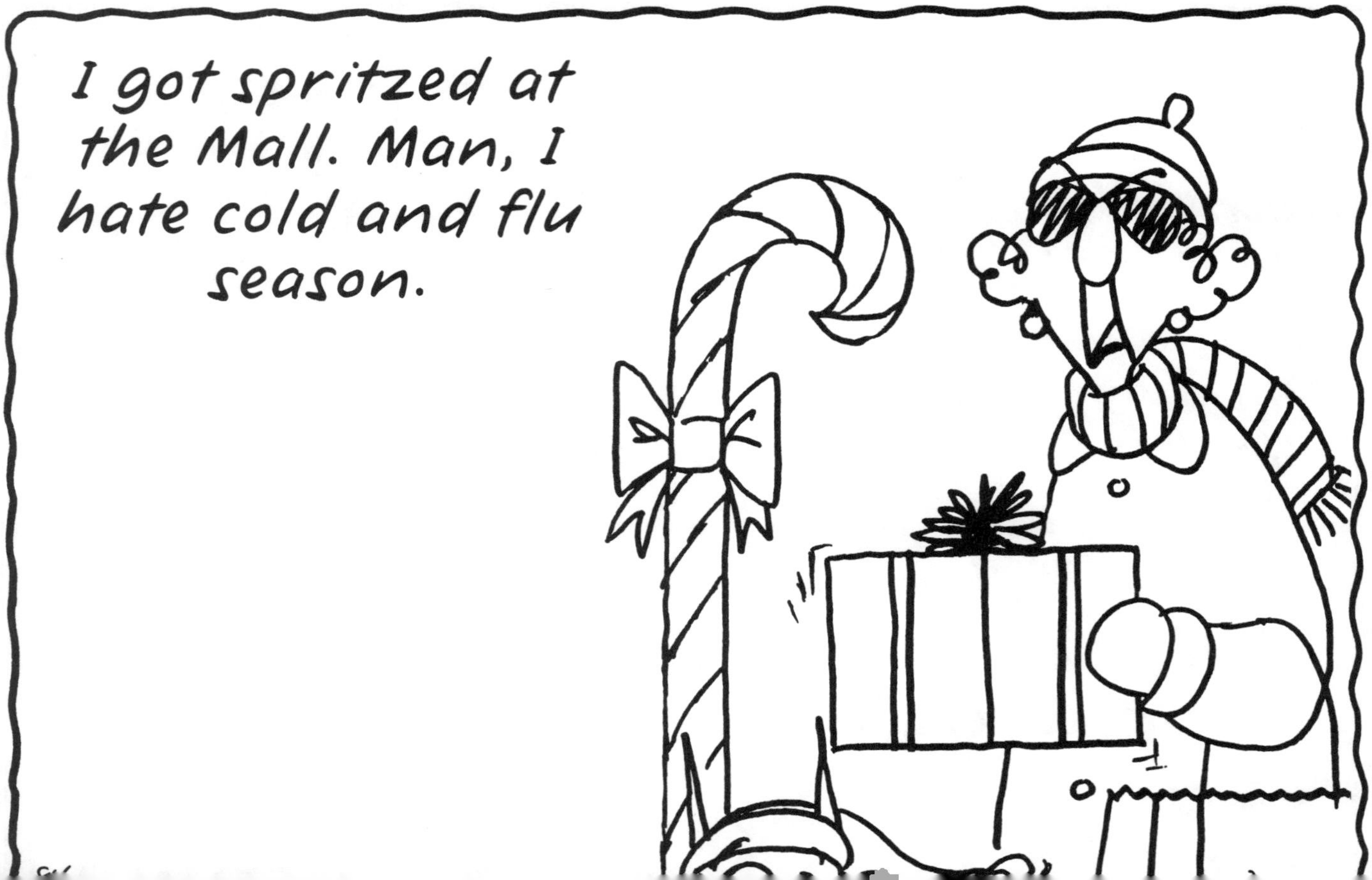
I got spritzed at the Mall. Man, I hate cold and flu season.

Every year I have to replace burned-out bulbs in my Christmas lights.

Luckily, my neighbors use the same size I do.

Every Christmas I think
about buying a new house...

All my relatives know where
this one is.

92

I always give
candy at
Christmas.

People have
to stop
singin'
to eat it.

94

It's Christmas, time for me to make gingerbread men modeled after my relatives.
Half-baked.